T0163084

Find it!
In the country

Published by Richardson Publishing Group Limited.
www.richardsonpublishinggroup.com

10 9 8 7 6 5 4 3 2 1

Design by Junior London Ltd, junior.london. Illustration by Jonathan Mortimer.

ISBN 978-1-913602-23-9

Printed and bound by Bell & Bain Ltd, 303 Burnfield Road, Thornliebank, Glasgow G46 7UQ.

The contents of this publication are believed correct at the time of printing. Nevertheless the publisher can accept no responsibility for errors, omissions, or changes in the detail given, or for any expense or loss thereby caused.

A catalogue record for this book is available from the British Library.

If you would like to comment on any aspect of this book, please contact us at:

E-mail: puzzles@richardsonpublishinggroup.com

🐦 Follow us on Twitter @puzzlesandgames
📷 instagram.com/richardsonpuzzlesandgames
f facebook.com/richardsonpuzzlesandgames

Contents

Introduction

Find it! books are designed to foster a love of learning and exploring the world through having fun.

Each of our books contain twenty-five things to find in the world around you, along with amazing facts and mind-bending puzzles.

Solutions to the puzzles can be found in the back of the book along with a place to make notes on your finds and a summary chart of the things to find. You can use the summary chart as an index to quickly locate your finds within the book or you can cut it out of the book and use it to find things on your travels!

Once you have found everything, there is a certificate at the very back of the book which you can ask a parent or guardian to complete and award to you!

For every 3 books completed, a parent or guardian can send us a message in order to receive a Find it! Super Spotter badge (T&Cs apply)! Simply fill in the form on our website at: richardsonpuzzlesandgames.com/superspotter

Happy finding!

Introduction

Tick this box when you have found the object. If you have a friend or sibling with you, why don't you set up a game to see who can find the most objects each?

Activity to complete!

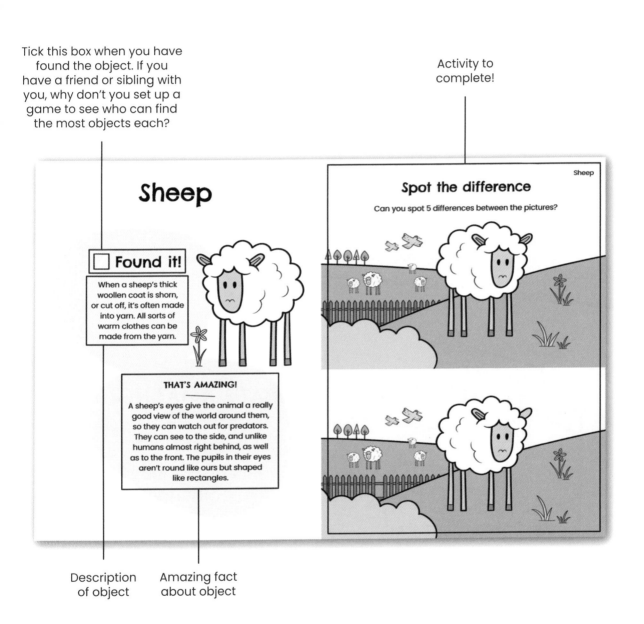

Sheep

☐ **Found it!**

When a sheep's thick woollen coat is shorn, or cut off, it's often made into yarn. All sorts of warm clothes can be made from the yarn.

THAT'S AMAZING!

A sheep's eyes give the animal a really good view of the world around them, so they can watch out for predators. They can see to the side, and unlike humans almost right behind, as well as to the front. The pupils in their eyes aren't round like ours but shaped like rectangles.

Spot the difference

Can you spot 5 differences between the pictures?

Sheep

Description of object

Amazing fact about object

Boots

☐ Found it!

Boots protect your feet and ankles, and they're usually waterproof, so they stop your feet from getting wet.

THAT'S AMAZING!

We've been wearing boots for a long time – cave paintings from more than 12,000 years ago show people wearing them!

Matching pairs

How many pairs of boots are there?

Pairs

Gate

☑ Found it!

Gates are made in walls and fences so that people can get in and out, but animals can't.

THAT'S AMAZING!

Hundreds of years ago, mighty walls were built around some cities, with huge gates to let visitors and citizens in and out. Some of them still stand today. The Brandenburg Gate in the city of Berlin, Germany, is 26 m (over 85 ft) high, supported by twelve massive columns.

Maze

Find the route that leads to the open gate.

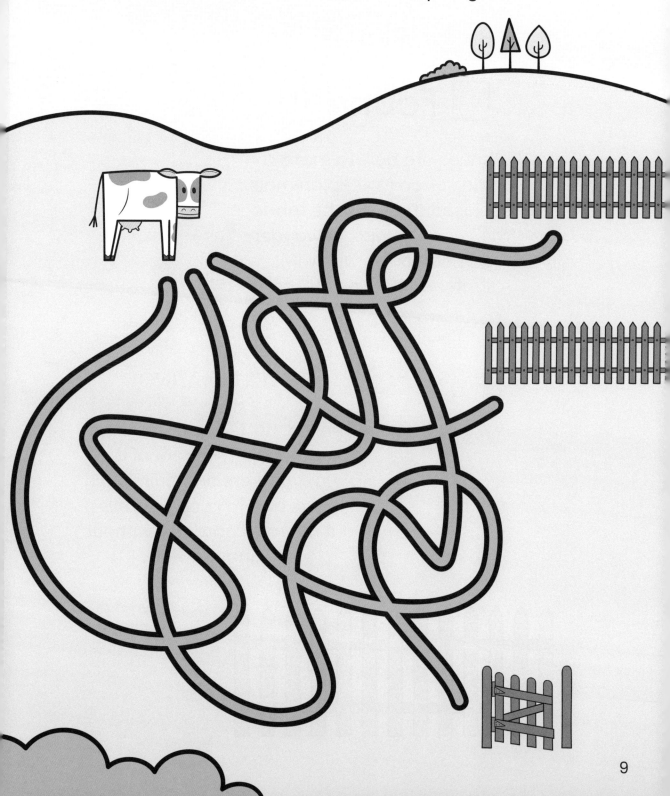

Fence

 Found it!

Fences are built to make a barrier, often to keep animals enclosed. They can be made from wood or wire, or wooden or metal posts with wires stretched between them.

THAT'S AMAZING!

The 'ha-ha' is a sunken fence with a ditch in front of it. Ha-has were first built 300 years ago to keep animals out of grand gardens, without spoiling the view.

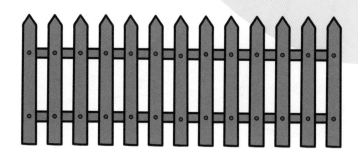

Group together

Draw a circle around all the cows in the
field without including any sheep.

Church

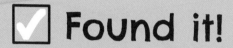 **Found it!**

Christianity is one of the world's many religions. Churches are places of worship for Christians.

THAT'S AMAZING!

St Peter's Basilica in Vatican City, Rome, Italy, is the biggest church on Earth. It covers roughly the same area as two city blocks.

Telling the time

The church service starts at 9 o'clock. How long is it until each service starts?

minutes   minutes   minutes

minutes   minutes

Barn

☐ Found it!

Barns are big farm
buildings. They can be
used to store grain,
farm tools, or animals.

THAT'S AMAZING!

———

Barns look different in different
parts of the world. In North
America they are often painted
red, because hundreds of years
ago farmers used oil mixed with
rust to paint them – the red rust
helped stop moss and fungus
from growing on the barn.

Wordsearch

Look for the 10 words hidden in the wordsearch puzzle. The hidden words will run down and across. There are no words that run backwards or on a diagonal.

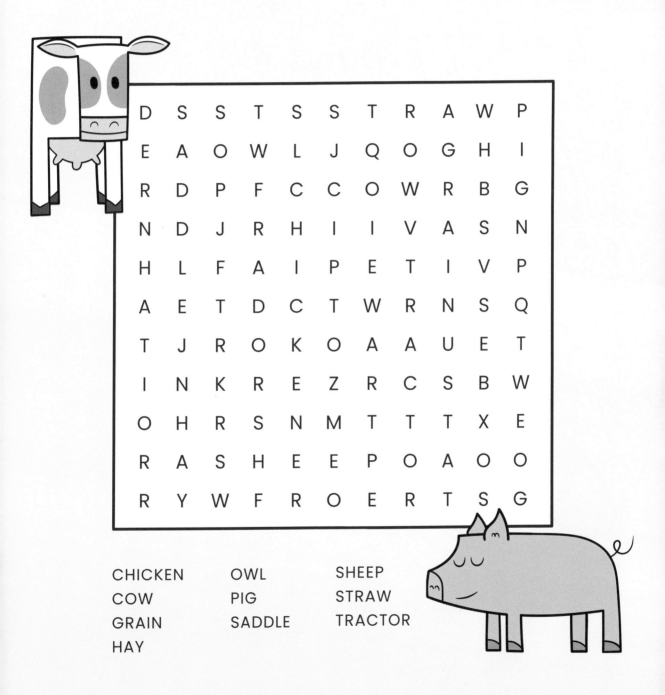

D	S	S	T	S	S	T	R	A	W	P
E	A	O	W	L	J	Q	O	G	H	I
R	D	P	F	C	C	O	W	R	B	G
N	D	J	R	H	I	I	V	A	S	N
H	L	F	A	I	P	E	T	I	V	P
A	E	T	D	C	T	W	R	N	S	Q
T	J	R	O	K	O	A	A	U	E	T
I	N	K	R	E	Z	R	C	S	B	W
O	H	R	S	N	M	T	T	T	X	E
R	A	S	H	E	E	P	O	A	O	O
R	Y	W	F	R	O	E	R	T	S	G

CHICKEN   OWL   SHEEP
COW   PIG   STRAW
GRAIN   SADDLE   TRACTOR
HAY

Crop field

☑ Found it!

Farmers grow the same kind of plant all together so that the whole field can be harvested at the same time. Many crops are grown for food, such as wheat, rice, fruit and vegetables. Crops are also grown to make oil or material for our clothes.

THAT'S AMAZING!

Corn, or maize, is the world's most popular food crop. The corn cob is part of the plant's flower, and each kernel is a seed.

Dot to dot

Trace the lines up and down while keeping your pen on the page. Make sure you get them as straight as you can!

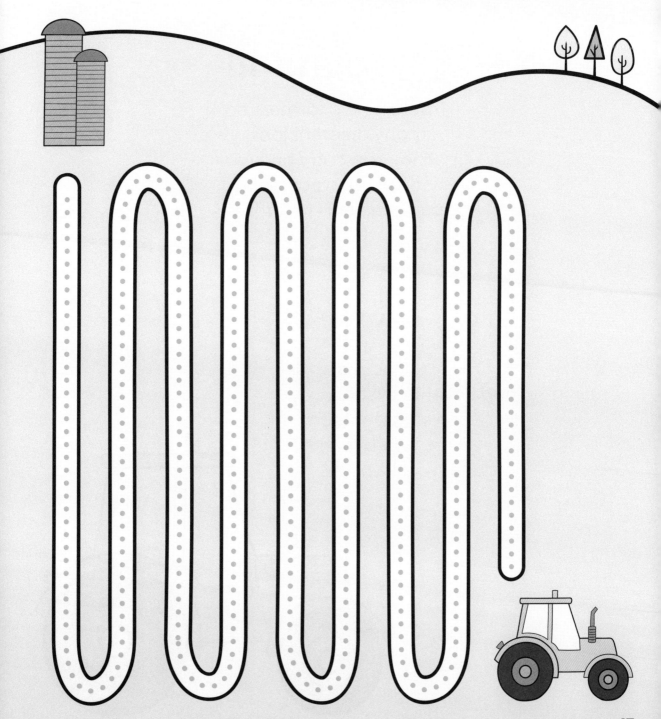

Tractor

☑ **Found it!**

Tractors help farmers do many different jobs. They can carry heavy loads, mow grass, and prepare fields for crops.

THAT'S AMAZING!

———

The first tractors, made over 100 years ago, were powered by steam. They were very big, with huge metal wheels.

Spot the difference

Can you spot 5 differences between the pictures?

Plane

☑ Found it!

Planes fly through the sky carrying people travelling for work or a holiday. Goods such as fruit and vegetables that need to be eaten quickly, are also flown in from far away places. Sometimes planes leave vapour trails on a clear day.

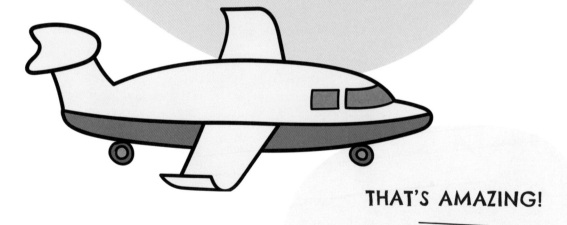

THAT'S AMAZING!

Around 100,000 flights take off every day all over the world.

Maze

Guide the plane to the airport parking space.

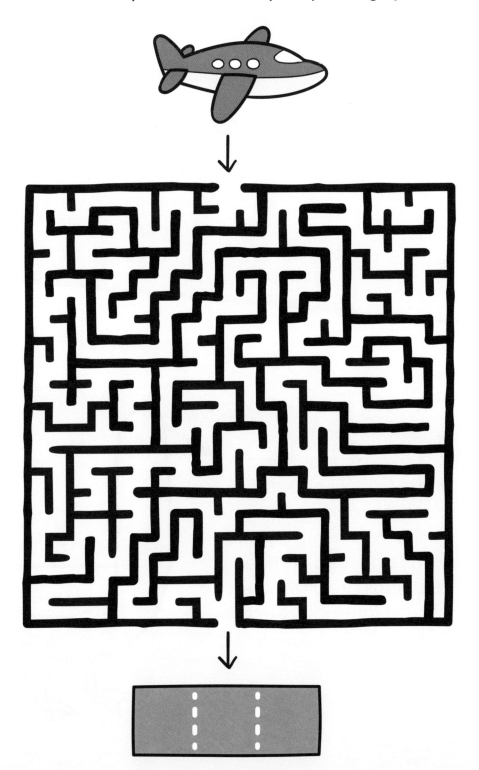

Flock of birds

 **Found it!**

Some birds fly in a group called a flock, all heading in the same direction and flying close together. You might see a flock of geese flying in a V-shape.

THAT'S AMAZING!

A 'murmuration' is a large flock of birds flying together, making patterns in the sky as they fly one way and then another. Starlings are often seen flying in formation like this.

Numbers

How many birds with three tail feathers are there in the flock?

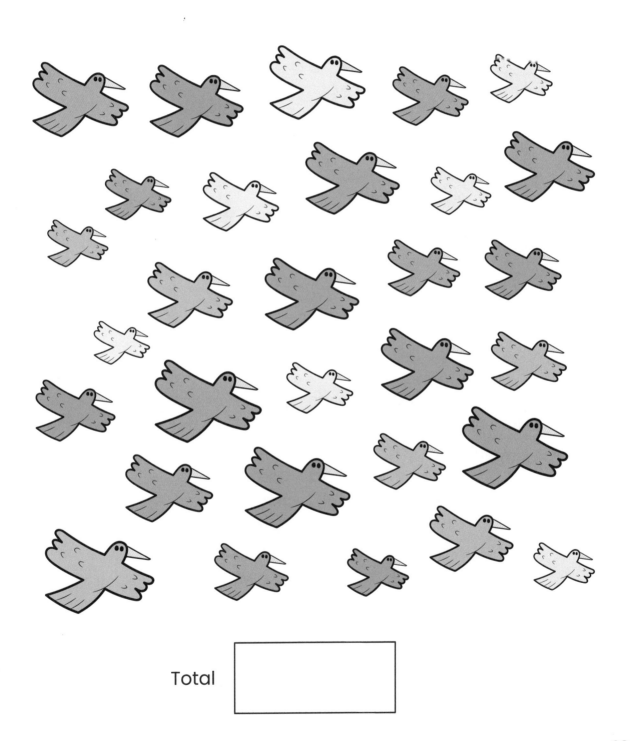

Total

Crow

☑ Found it!

There are different kinds of crow, including rooks, ravens and jackdaws. Most have black feathers.

THAT'S AMAZING!

Crows are surprisingly clever. A group of carrion crows in Japan has learned to read traffic lights – when the lights are red, the crows leave nuts on the road, and when the lights are green the cars run the nuts over and crack them. The crows wait for the lights to turn red again, then pick up and eat the nuts!

Complete the picture

Draw the other half of the crow.

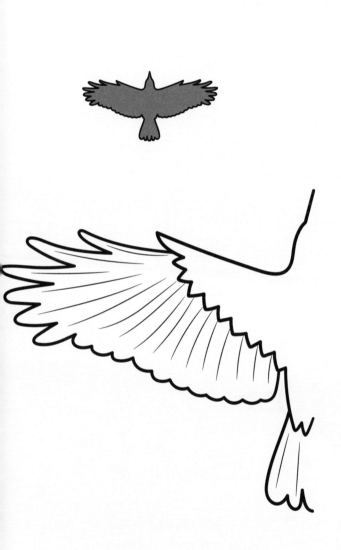

Duck

☑ Found it!

Ducks spend their time on or near water. They have webbed feet for swimming, and the waxy outer feathers are so good at keeping out water that the soft, downy feathers next to the ducks' skin always stay dry and warm.

THAT'S AMAZING!

Ducks' feet don't feel the cold, so they don't mind swimming in icy water or walking across snow.

Dot to dot

Connect the dots to uncover a picture,
then fill in with pens or pencils.

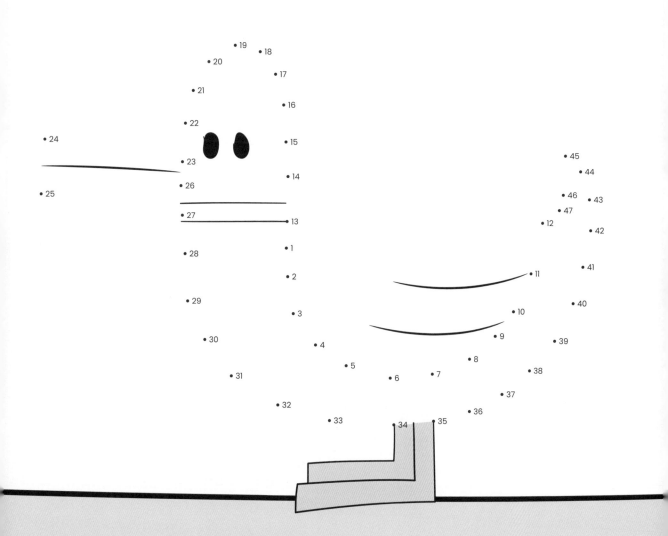

Rabbit

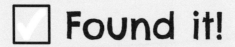 **Found it!**

In the wild, rabbits live in large groups in underground burrows. A network of burrows is called a rabbit warren.

THAT'S AMAZING!

Baby rabbits are 'kits', female rabbits are 'does', and male rabbits are called 'bucks'.

Maze

Guide the rabbit through the warren to the carrot.

Sheep

☑ Found it!

When a sheep's thick woollen coat is shorn, or cut off, it's often made into yarn. All sorts of warm clothes can be made from the yarn.

THAT'S AMAZING!

A sheep's eyes give the animal a really good view of the world around them, so they can watch out for predators. They can see to the side, and unlike humans almost right behind, as well as to the front. The pupils in their eyes aren't round like ours but shaped like rectangles.

Spot the difference

Can you spot 5 differences between the pictures?

Dog

☑ Found it!

There are many different breeds of dog, from tiny Chihuahuas to huge English Mastiffs. They are very popular pets, and can also be trained to do useful things for people, like herding sheep, or helping people with vision or hearing loss.

THAT'S AMAZING!

Dogs have an amazing sense of smell – it's more than 10,000 times better than our own!

Wordsearch

Look for the 10 words hidden in the wordsearch puzzle. The hidden words will run down and across. There are no words that run backwards or on a diagonal.

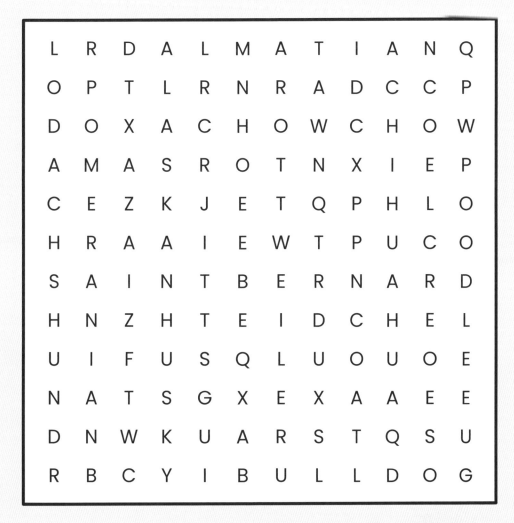

L	R	D	A	L	M	A	T	I	A	N	Q
O	P	T	L	R	N	R	A	D	C	C	P
D	O	X	A	C	H	O	W	C	H	O	W
A	M	A	S	R	O	T	N	X	I	E	P
C	E	Z	K	J	E	T	Q	P	H	L	O
H	R	A	A	I	E	W	T	P	U	C	O
S	A	I	N	T	B	E	R	N	A	R	D
H	N	Z	H	T	E	I	D	C	H	E	L
U	I	F	U	S	Q	L	U	O	U	O	E
N	A	T	S	G	X	E	X	A	A	E	E
D	N	W	K	U	A	R	S	T	Q	S	U
R	B	C	Y	I	B	U	L	L	D	O	G

ALASKAN HUSKY   POMERANIAN
BULLDOG   POODLE
CHIHUAHUA   ROTTWEILER
CHOW CHOW   SAINT BERNARD
DALMATIAN

Animal tracks

☐ Found it!

Animals leave tracks behind if
they walk in soft ground,
like mud, or through snow.
You can learn to identify the
animal that left the tracks.

THAT'S AMAZING!

———

There are animal tracks
millions of years old!
The footprints of dinosaurs
and other prehistoric
creatures can be preserved
in rock. One dinosaur track
measures 1.7 m (5 ft 9 in).
It must have been left by an
enormous sauropod dinosaur.

Matching pair

Circle the two animal tracks that are the same.

Muddy puddle

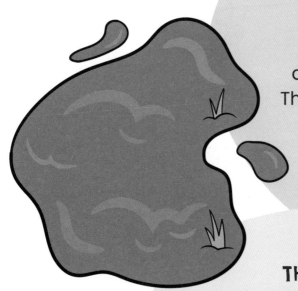

☑ Found it!

After heavy rain there
are lots of muddy puddles.
They're great fun to splash in,
if you don't mind
getting dirty!

THAT'S AMAZING!

There are plenty of puddles
in the town of Mawsynram
in India, which holds the
world record for the wettest
place on Earth. Every year,
around 1187.1 cm (467.4 in)
of rain falls there.

Complete the words

Can you complete the names of these animals that love muddy puddles? The images next to the words are a clue. Cover them up if you would like to make the puzzle harder!

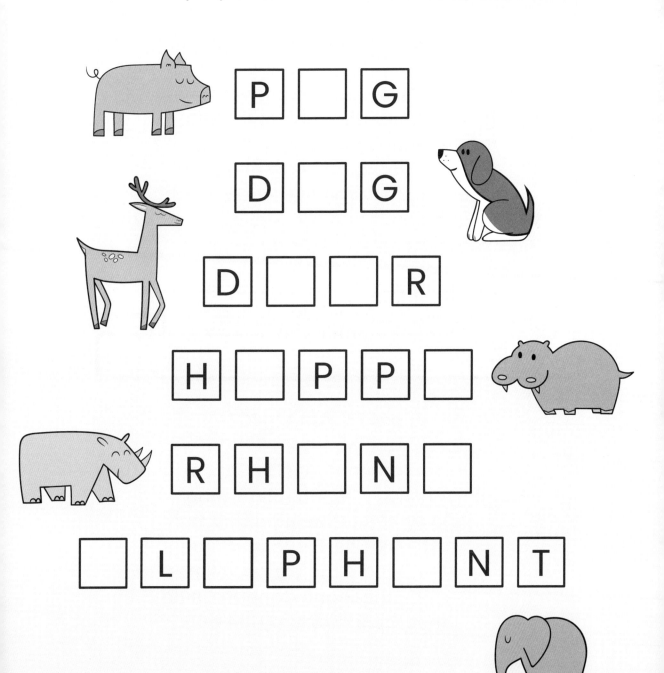

P ☐ G

D ☐ G

D ☐ ☐ R

H ☐ P P ☐

R H ☐ N ☐

☐ L ☐ P H ☐ N T

River

☑ Found it!

Rivers run from a source, sometimes high up in the mountains, to the sea. Before there were trains or trucks, artificial rivers called canals were built to move heavy goods. Canals have also been built to make useful shortcuts for ships.

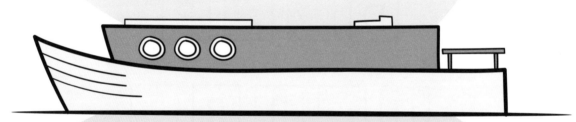

THAT'S AMAZING!

The Panama Canal in Central America is 82 km (51 mi) long, and connects the Atlantic Ocean with the Pacific. The longest canal in the world is more than 21 times longer – the Grand Canal in China measures 1,776 km (1,104 mi).

Maze

Help the boat to find the river that leads to the landing.

Seed

☑ Found it!

Plants form seeds to make new plants – every seed is waiting to be a whole new plant! A nut is a seed – the tough shell surrounds the seed inside, and many of them are good to eat.

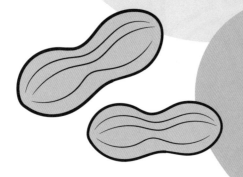

THAT'S AMAZING!

Peanuts aren't really nuts at all. They don't grow on trees, and are related to peas and beans.

Numbers

What is the difference between the number of nuts in the tree and on the floor? Use the number line if you need it.

Purple flower

☑ Found it!

Thistles are spiky plants with purple or pink flowers. The prickles protect the plant from animals that might want to eat them.

THAT'S AMAZING!
***
The thistle is the national flower of Scotland.

Draw a picture

What purple flowers can you find? Draw them here.

Berry

☑ Found it!

Berries are fruit, and many of them, such as blueberries and gooseberries, are delicious to eat.

THAT'S AMAZING!

Not all berries are tasty, and some are dangerous. For example, red holly berries look good but are poisonous.

Wordsearch

Look for the 10 words hidden in the wordsearch puzzle. The hidden words will run down and across. There are no words that run backwards or on a diagonal.

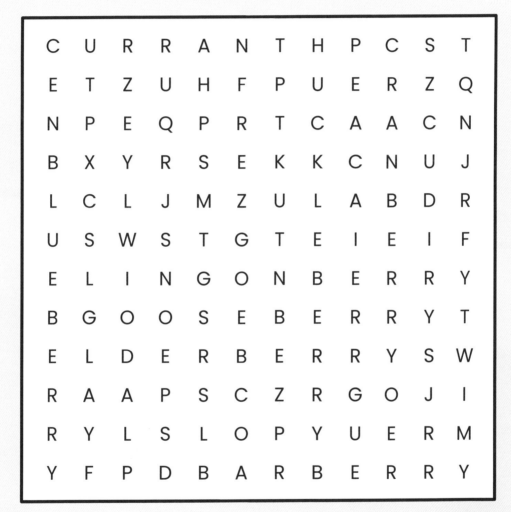

```
C U R R A N T H P C S T
E T Z U H F P U E R Z Q
N P E Q P R T C A A C N
B X Y R S E K K C N U J
L C L J M Z U L A B D R
U S W S T G T E I E I F
E L I N G O N B E R R Y
B G O O S E B E R R Y T
E L D E R B E R R Y S W
R A A P S C Z R G O J I
R Y L S L O P Y U E R M
Y F P D B A R B E R R Y
```

ACAI
BARBERRY
BLUEBERRY
CRANBERRY

CURRANT
ELDERBERRY
GOJI

GOOSEBERRY
HUCKLEBERRY
LINGONBERRY

Red or pink flower

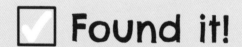 Found it!

Poppies have beautiful, papery flowers, which can be red, pink, orange, or even white! They often grow wild at the edges of fields. Lots of different kinds of poppy are grown as garden plants.

THAT'S AMAZING!

A single poppy plant can make more than 50,000 seeds!

Draw a picture

What red or pink flowers can you find? Draw them here.

Mushroom

☑ Found it!

There are hundreds of different kinds of mushroom, which is a type of fungus. Some mushrooms are good to eat, some are poisonous, and some glow in the dark!

THAT'S AMAZING!

Fungi (more than one fungus) are not plants or animals – they are a group of living things that includes yeasts and mushrooms, many of which are too small to see without a microscope.

Spot the difference

Circle the odd one out.

Yellow flower

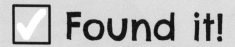

☑ **Found it!**

Daffodils are cheerful spring flowers that are usually yellow, orange or white.

THAT'S AMAZING!

Narcissus is another word for a daffodil. Narcissus was also the name of a young man in Ancient Greek mythology, who was so beautiful that he fell in love with his own reflection.

Draw a picture

What yellow flowers can you find? Draw them here.

Tree

☑ **Found it!**

Trees are tall plants. They all have leaves – deciduous trees' leaves fall off in winter and grow again in spring; evergreen trees keep their leaves all year round. Trees are home to animals, including birds, squirrels, monkeys and insects.

THAT'S AMAZING!

There are tens of thousands of different kinds of tree. They cover one third of the whole world.

Complete the words

Complete the names of these types of fruit trees. The images next to the words are a clue. Cover them up if you would like to make the puzzle harder!

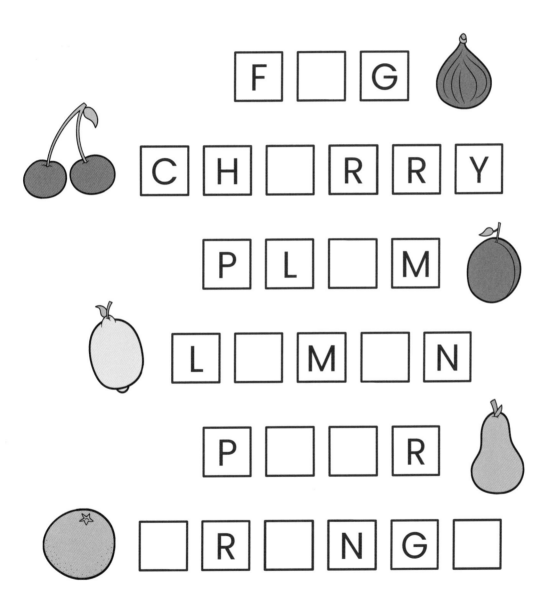

F ☐ G

C H ☐ R R Y

P L ☐ M

L ☐ M ☐ N

P ☐ ☐ R

☐ R ☐ N G ☐

Moss

☑ Found it!

You often see mosses growing on trees, walls and roofs. They are green plants with stems and leaves but no flowers.

THAT'S AMAZING!

Mosses are ancient – they have been living on Earth for 450 million years – long before the time of the dinosaurs!

Dot to dot

Connect the dots to uncover a picture,
then fill in with pens or pencils.

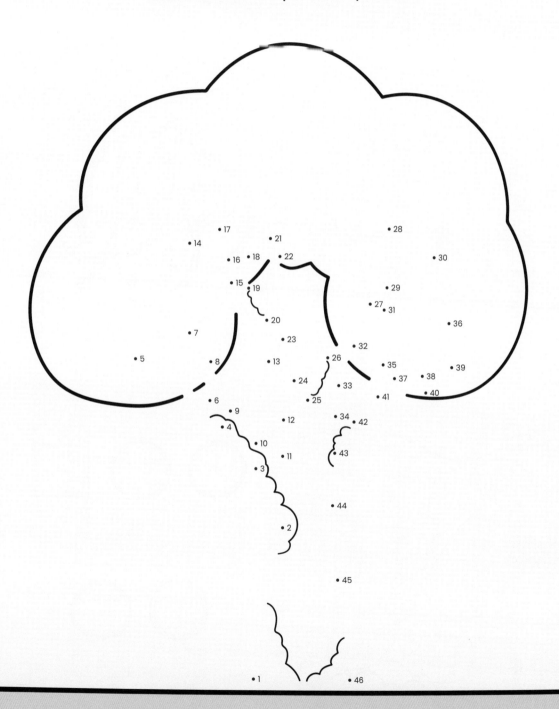

Solutions

Page 07

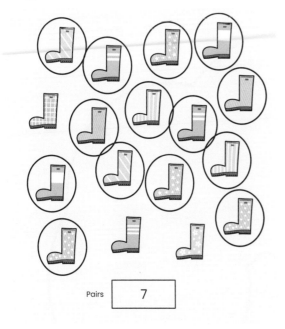

Pairs | 7

Page 09

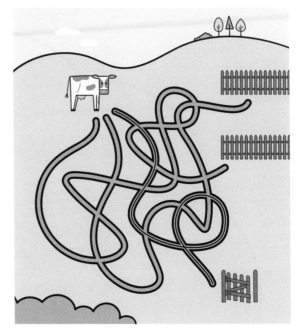

Page 11

Page 13

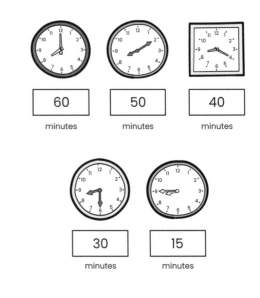

60 minutes

50 minutes

40 minutes

30 minutes

15 minutes

Solutions

Page 15

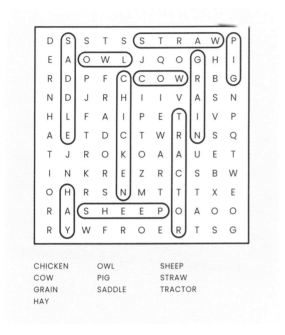

CHICKEN   OWL   SHEEP
COW   PIG   STRAW
GRAIN   SADDLE   TRACTOR
HAY

Page 19

Page 21

Page 23

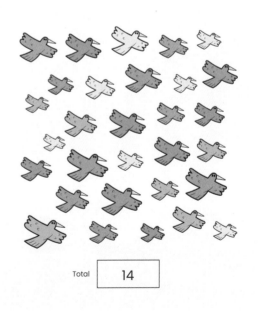

Total   14

Solutions

Page 27

Page 29

Page 31

Page 33

ALASKAN HUSKY   POMERANIAN
BULLDOG   POODLE
CHIHUAHUA   ROOTWEILER
CHOW CHOW   SAINT BERNARD
DALMATION

Solutions

Page 35

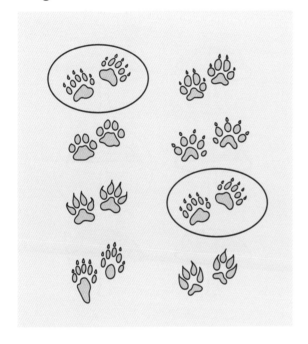

Page 37

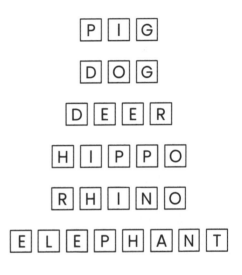

Page 39

Page 41

Solutions

Page 45

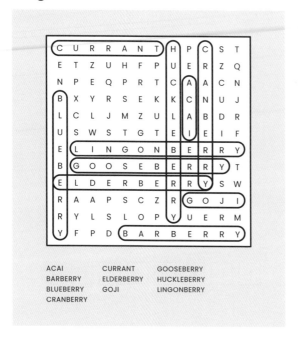

ACAI
BARBERRY
BLUEBERRY
CRANBERRY

CURRANT
ELDERBERRY
GOJI

GOOSEBERRY
HUCKLEBERRY
LINGONBERRY

Page 49

Page 53

Page 55

Notes on my finds

_____

_____

_____

_____

_____

_____

_____

_____

_____

_____

_____

_____

_____

_____

Notes on my finds

Chart of my finds

Finds by:

....

Use this chart as an index to quickly locate your finds within the book, or you can cut it out of the book and use it to find things on your travels. An adult can also use this page to confirm your finds!

Animal tracks	☐	p.34	Flock of birds	☐	p.22
Barn	☐	p.14	Gate	☐	p.08
Berry	☐	p.44	Moss	☐	p.54
Boots	☐	p.06	Muddy puddle	☐	p.36
Church	☐	p.12	Mushroom	☐	p.48
Crop field	☐	p.16	Plane	☐	p.20
Crow	☐	p.24	Rabbit	☐	p.28
Dog	☐	p.32	River	☐	p.38
Duck	☐	p.26	Seed	☐	p.40
Fence	☐	p.10	Sheep	☐	p.30
Flower, purple	☐	p.42	Tractor	☐	p.18
Flower, red/pink	☐	p.46	Tree	☐	p.52
Flower, yellow	☐	p.50			

Find it!

Certificate

This certificate is awarded to:

....

For completing:

Find it! In the country

....

Date: ....